# How silly!

**Story written by Gill Munton**
**Illustrated by Tim Archbold**

# Speed Sounds

## Consonants   *Ask children to say the sounds.*

| f | l | m | n | r | s | v | z | sh | th | ng |
|---|---|---|---|---|---|---|---|---|---|---|
| ff | ll | mm | nn | rr | ss | **ve** | zz | | | nk |
| ph | le | mb | kn | **wr** | se | | **se** | | | |
| | | | gn | | c | | s | | | |
| | | | | | ce | | | | | |

| b | c | d | g | h | j | p | qu | t | w | x | y | ch |
|---|---|---|---|---|---|---|---|---|---|---|---|---|
| bb | k | dd | gg | | g | pp | | tt | wh | | | **tch** |
| | ck | | gu | | ge | | | | | | | |

*Each box contains one sound but sometimes more than one grapheme.*
*Focus graphemes for this story are **circled**.*

## Vowels    *Ask children to say the sounds in and out of order.*

| a | e<br>ea | i | o | u | ay<br>a͡-e<br>a | ee<br>ea<br>y<br>e | igh<br>i͡-e<br>ie<br>i | ow<br>o͡-e<br>o<br>oe |
|---|---|---|---|---|---|---|---|---|
| at | hen | in | on | up | day | see | high | blow |

| oo<br>u͡-e<br>ue | oo | ar | or<br>oor<br>ore<br>aw | air<br>are | ir<br>ur<br>er | ou<br>ow | oy<br>oi |
|---|---|---|---|---|---|---|---|
| zoo | look | car | for | fair | whirl | shout | boy |

# Story Green Words

*Ask children to read the words first in Fred Talk and then say the word.*

Barbara   Howard   beam   howl   inn   drown

---

*Ask children to say the syllables and then read the whole word.*

cell|ar   hope|less   farm|house   night|gown   stock|ings

caul|i|flow|er*

---

*Ask children to read the root first and then the whole word with the suffix.*

crouch → crouched   silly → silliest   bow → bowed

polite → politely   frown → frowned   share → shared

cloud → clouds   part → parted   gather → gathered

*\* Challenge Words*

# Vocabulary Check

*Discuss the meaning (as used in the story) after the children have read each word.*

| | definition: | sentence: |
|---|---|---|
| **cellar** | room under the house | "Go down to the cellar and fetch me some flour." |
| **beam** | strong wood | He saw a big cooking pot hanging from the beam above his head. |
| **crouched** | bent down | He crouched down. |
| **inn** | a hotel | She came to a town, and stopped at an inn for the night. |
| **stockings** | long socks | She found that Rose had tied her stockings to some coat pegs. |

# Red Words

| | | | |
|---|---|---|---|
| above | father | son | mother |
| some | here | who | there |
| people | water | was | to |
| you | all | what | come |
| they | were | one | should |

8

# How silly!

Bossy Barbara was visiting Hopeless Howard.
She was helping Howard's mother make
cauliflower cheese.

"Go down to the cellar and fetch me
some flour, Howard," Barbara shouted.

As Howard was about to bring
the flour up to the kitchen,
he saw a big cooking pot hanging from a beam above his head.

He crouched down and began to howl:

"What if I marry Barbara,

and we have a son,

and our son grows up,

and I send him down here for flour ...

and that cooking pot falls down and

knocks him out?"

Howard's mother and father came down to look for him.
When he told them what was wrong, they began to howl, too.

The noise was so loud that Barbara came down.

When they told her what was wrong, she said: "How silly you all sound! I can't marry the silliest man in the land!

I'm going to see if I can find three sillies who are even sillier than you! Then I will come back and marry Howard!"

Off Barbara went.

First, she came to a farmhouse
with grass growing on the roof.
A man was pushing a cow up a ladder!

Barbara bowed politely, and asked him why.

"The best grass is on my roof," he frowned,
"so I've got to get the cow up there to eat it."

That was the first silly.

Barbara went on her way.
She came to a town, and stopped
at an inn for the night.
She shared a room with a girl called Rose.

In the morning, Barbara took off her nightgown,
had a shower and dried herself with a towel.

When she came out of the bathroom,
she found that Rose had tied her stockings
to some coat pegs and was trying to jump into them!

That was the second silly.

As Barbara left the town,
the clouds parted and the sun came out.
She saw a crowd of people gathered round a pond.

A boy was dipping a net into the water.

"The sun has fallen into the pond!" he shouted.
"I must get it out – or it will drown!"

"There's no doubt about it," smiled Barbara,
counting on her fingers, "now I have found
my three sillies!"

So she went back to Howard,
and they were married,
and they did have a son.

One day, when the son was
grown up, Howard did send him down
to the cellar to fetch some flour.
And the cooking pot did fall down ...

but it missed him!

# Questions to talk about

*Ask children to TTYP each question using 'Fastest finger' (FF) or 'Have a think' (HaT).*

**p.9** (FF) What did Howard see hanging from a beam?

**p.10** (FF) What was Howard worried about?

**p.11** (HaT) Why did Barbara want to wait before she married Howard?

**p.12** (FF) Why was the man trying to push a cow up a ladder?

**p.13** (FF) What had Rose tied her stockings to?

**p.14** (FF) What did the boy think would happen to the sun if he didn't get it out of the pond?

**p.15** (HaT) What did you think when the cooking pot fell down at the end of the story?

# Questions to read and answer

*(Children complete without your help.)*

1. Why did Howard go down to the cellar?

2. Why was Howard (and his mother and father) upset?

3. What was the first 'silly' doing?

4. Which 'silly' do you think was the silliest? Explain.

5. What is funny about the story at the end?

# Speedy Green Words

*Ask children to practise reading the words across the rows, down the columns and in and out of order clearly and quickly.*

| | | | |
|---|---|---|---|
| fetch | shout | noise | shout |
| land | coat | doubt | coat |
| make | night | kitchen | began |
| wrong | first | girl | round |
| stopped | found | pushing | silly |